MEL BAY PRESENTS

BLUES GUITAR
MADE EASY
BY COREY CHRISTIANSEN

CD Contents

MEL BAY ®

1 2 3 4 5 6 7 8 9 0

© 2004 BY MEL BAY PUBLICATIONS, INC., PACIFIC, MO 63069.
ALL RIGHTS RESERVED. INTERNATIONAL COPYRIGHT SECURED. B.M.I. MADE AND PRINTED IN U.S.A.

Visit us on the Web at www.melbay.com — E-mail us at email@melbay.com

Table of Contents

Introduction

When I was in college I taught about 60 private students a week, many of whom were beginners who wanted to play the blues. While there were a number of great blues methods available, many of which contained a number of tunes for students to play, there wasn't a collection of easy graded solos for students to play. This book contains a number of easy blues solos written for the beginning blues guitarist. Many of the solos are to be played in the first position but a few of them are in the third and higher positions.

All of the solos in this collection are presented in standard notation and tab. Students should read the standard notation as much as their reading skills will allow as that is where the rhythmic notation is contained, but the tab will allow any student to play the solos in higher positions where many beginners find reading challenging. Many of the solos have techniques written such as slides, 1/4 step bends (a very slight bend), and grace notes. These are simple techniques to execute and can be mimicked by listening to the play-along recording if the student does not read these techniques in standard notation.

Use the play-along CD as you practice. A professional band has recorded each tune. This will help students hear the groove of the tune and how each piece should be phrased. Historically, the blues is an aural tradition and many of the most prolific blues artists learned by ear. The CD will provide invaluable help for playing these tunes authentically. Most of all have fun with this collection of blues music.

Corey

Blues Only

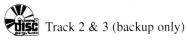 Track 2 & 3 (backup only)

Da' Blues

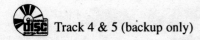

Blues Outa the Gate

Blues Annex

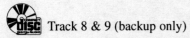

Track 8 & 9 (backup only)

Blues 2 Annex

Track 10 & 11 (backup only)

No Way Out

Track 12 & 13 (backup only)

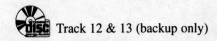

Yeah Baby

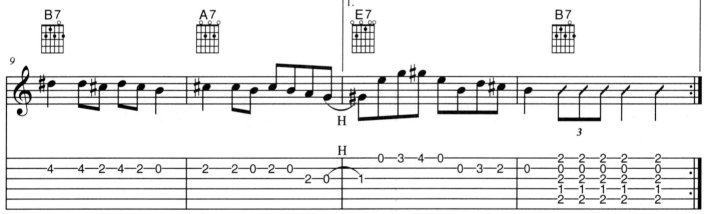

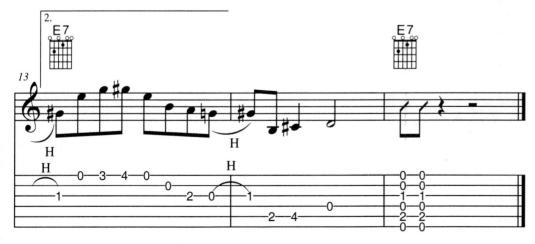

11

Nothin' Bitin'

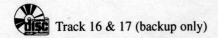 

Track 16 & 17 (backup only)

12

This page has been left blank
to avoid awkward page turns.

What it Is

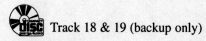

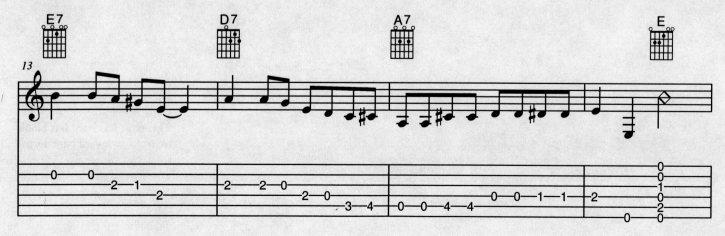

Hot Sauce Boogie

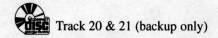

Track 20 & 21 (backup only)

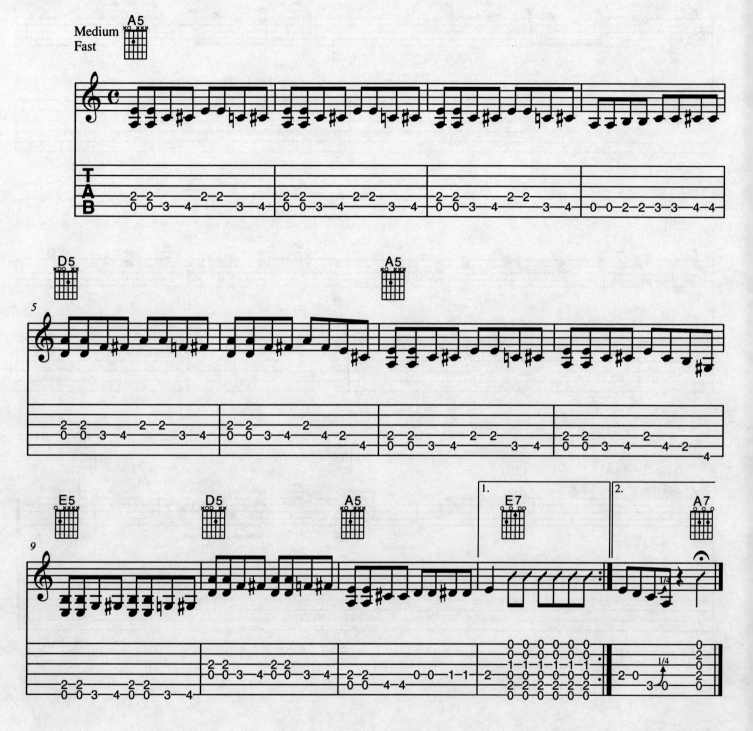

G Baby

Track 22 & 23 (backup only)

Minor Inconvenience

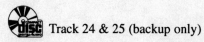

Track 24 & 25 (backup only)

This page has been left blank
to avoid awkward page turns.

Say What

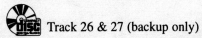

Track 26 & 27 (backup only)

South Side

Track 28 & 29 (backup only)

About the Author

Corey Christiansen began playing the guitar at the age of five. He studied with his father, Mike Christiansen, (a seasoned performer, writer, and educator at Utah State University) until he finished his bachelor degree. While at Utah State University, Corey received many honors and awards including the outstanding music student award and outstanding guitarist. The Lionel Hampton Jazz Festival awarded Corey with outstanding big band guitarist in 1995 and outstanding solo guitarist in 1995 and 1996.

Seeking a masters degree in jazz performance, Corey sought out renowned jazz guitar educator, Jack Petersen and began studies as a graduate teaching assistant at the University of South Florida. He received his masters degree in jazz performance in the spring of 1999. Jack Petersen retired that same year and Corey was hired to take his place as the adjunct guitar instructor. While teaching at the University of South Florida, Corey worked with the jazz guitar students and directed many of the jazz combos.

Corey left USF to pursue a career at Mel Bay Publications, Inc. as their guitar editor. Corey has a musical background covering many styles of music including jazz, blues, classical, bluegrass, folk, rock and popular music. This quality has enabled him to perform in a number of different settings. As the guitar editor at Mel Bay Publications, Inc., Corey is available to do clinics on various guitar related subjects at schools and music stores around the country.

Check out Corey's WebSite @ www.coreychristiansen.com

EXCELLENCE IN MUSIC

MEL BAY®

Since 1947